# Easy Concertos
# and Concertinos

## for Violin and Piano

# O. Rieding

# Concerto

## in B minor

# Op.35

### (1st position)

# BOSWORTH

# Concert in H moll.
## Concerto in B minor.

O. Rieding, Op. 35.

Violin, Viola or 'Cello

Piano.

Copyright 1909 by Bosworth & Cᵒ

B. & Cᵒ 13331

8

# Easy Concertos and Concertinos

for Violin and Piano

# O. Rieding

# Concerto

in B minor

# Op. 35

(1st position)

**Bosworth**

# Concert in H moll.
## Concerto in B minor.

### SOLO VIOLIN
(or 1st Violin in String (or Full) Orchestra)

O. Rieding, Op. 35.

**Allegro moderato.**

B. & Cº 13331

*Tous droits d'exécution réservés*

# Violine.

B. & CO 13331

# Violine.

# Violine.

# Violine.

# Violine.

B. & Cº 13331

Printed and bound in Great Britain by
Caligraving Limited Thetford Norfolk

4/10(173829)

## STRING ORCHESTRA     STREICHORCHESTER
## ORCHESTRE A CORDES     ORCHESTRA D'ARCHI

The following concertos and concertinos from the list are available with full string orchestral accompaniment:

Nachstehende Konzerte und Concertinos aus unserem Angebot sind mit voller Streichorchester-Begleitung lieferbar:

Les concertos et les concertinos de la liste suivante sont disponibles avec leur accompagnement d'orchestre à cordes:

I seguenti concerti e concertini come da lista sono disponibili con accompagnamento d'orchestra d'archi:

このリストにあるコンチェルトとコンチェルティノスは
すべて完全なストリング・オーケストラの伴奏付きです。

| | | | | | |
|---|---|---|---|---|---|
| * Kuchler | Opus 12 | * Portnoff | Opus 13 | Seitz | Opus 15 |
| * Kuchler | Opus 15 | Rieding | Opus 34 | Seitz | Opus 22 |
| * Millies | (In the style of Mozart) | * Rieding | Opus 35 | Ten Have | Opus 30 |

**SELECTED PIECES FROM HANDEL** edited by Felix Borowski

**AUSGEWÄHLTE STÜCKE VON HÄNDEL** herausgegeben von Felix Borowski

**PIECES CHOISIES DE HAENDEL** éditées par Félix Borowski

**SELEZIONI DI PEZZI DI HÄNDEL** curate da Felix Borowski

ヘンデル小品集 フェリックス・ボロウスキ 校閲

Bourree    Gavotte    Hornpipe    Largo    Menuet    Musette    Sarabande

**\*SIX VERY EASY PIECES in the First Position** by Edward Elgar

**\*SECHS SEHR LEICHTE STÜCKE in der Ersten Lage** von Edward Elgar

**\*SIX PIECES TRES FACILES dans la Première Position** d'Edward Elgar

**\*SEI PEZZI MOLTO FACILI in Prima Posizione** di Edward Elgar

\* やさしい小品6曲集 ファースト・ポジション エドワード・エルガー 校閲

All these are available with Piano, 1st Violin, 2nd Violin, 3rd Elementary Violin, 4th Violin (in lieu of Viola), Viola, 'Cello and Double Bass.
   \* Also with additional parts for woodwind, brass and percussion.

Alle angeführten Werke lieferbar mit Klavier, 1. Violine, 2. Violine, 3. Violine (Obligat), 4. Violine (an Stelle von Viola), Viola, 'Cello und Kontrabaß.
   \* auch mit zusätzlichen Stimmen für Holzblasinstrumente, Blechbläser und Schlagzeug.

Tous sont disponibles avec piano, 1er violon, 2ème violon, 3ème violon (élémentaire), 4ème violon (à la place de l'alto), alto, violoncelle et contrebasse.
   \* Disponibles aussi avec les parties supplémentaires de bois, cuivres et percussions.

Tutti questi pezzi sono disponibili per pianoforte, primo violino, secondo violino, terzo violino semplice, quarto violino (al posto della viola), viola, violoncello e contrabasso.
   \* anche con parti aggiuntive per strumenti a fiato, ottoni e strumenti a percussione.

これらはすべて、ピアノ、第1バイオリン、第2バイオリン、
第3エリメンタリー・バイオリン、第4バイオリン、ビオラ、
チェロ、ダブルベースのパート付きです。

   \* ウッドウインド、ブラス、パーカッションのパートもあります。

# BOSWORTH

Order No: BOE 003557

Allegro moderato.

Allegro moderato.

14

B. & Cᵒ 13331

Printed and bound in Great Britain by
Caligraving Limited Thetford Norfolk

4/10(173829)

# STRING ORCHESTRA    STREICHORCHESTER
## ORCHESTRE A CORDES    ORCHESTRA D'ARCHI

The following concertos and concertinos from the list are available with full string orchestral accompaniment:

Nachstehende Konzerte und Concertinos aus unserem Angebot sind mit voller Streichorchester-Begleitung lieferbar:

Les concertos et les concertinos de la liste suivante sont disponibles avec leur accompagnement d'orchestre à cordes:

I seguenti concerti e concertini come da lista sono disponibili con accompagnamento d'orchestra d'archi:

このリストにあるコンチェルトとコンチェルティノスは
すべて完全なストリング・オーケストラの伴奏付きです。

| | | | | | |
|---|---|---|---|---|---|
| *Kuchler | Opus 12 | *Portnoff | Opus 13 | Seitz | Opus 15 |
| *Kuchler | Opus 15 | Rieding | Opus 34 | Seitz | Opus 22 |
| *Millies | (In the style of Mozart) | *Rieding | Opus 35 | Ten Have | Opus 30 |

**SELECTED PIECES FROM HANDEL** edited by Felix Borowski

**AUSGEWÄHLTE STÜCKE VON HÄNDEL** herausgegeben von Felix Borowski

**PIECES CHOISIES DE HAENDEL** éditées par Félix Borowski

**SELEZIONI DI PEZZI DI HÄNDEL** curate da Felix Borowski

ヘンデル小品集 フェリックス・ボロウスキ 校閲

Bourree    Gavotte    Hornpipe    Largo    Menuet    Musette    Sarabande

**\*SIX VERY EASY PIECES in the First Position** by Edward Elgar

**\*SECHS SEHR LEICHTE STÜCKE in der Ersten Lage** von Edward Elgar

**\*SIX PIECES TRES FACILES dans la Première Position** d'Edward Elgar

**\*SEI PEZZI MOLTO FACILI in Prima Posizione** di Edward Elgar

＊やさしい小品6曲集 ファースト・ポジション エドワード・エルガー 校閲

All these are available with Piano, 1st Violin, 2nd Violin, 3rd Elementary Violin, 4th Violin (in lieu of Viola), Viola, 'Cello and Double Bass.
   * Also with additional parts for woodwind, brass and percussion.

Alle angeführten Werke lieferbar mit Klavier, 1. Violine, 2. Violine, 3. Violine (Obligat), 4. Violine (an Stelle von Viola), Viola, 'Cello und Kontrabaß.
   * auch mit zusätzlichen Stimmen für Holzblasinstrumente, Blechbläser und Schlagzeug.

Tous sont disponibles avec piano, 1er violon, 2ème violon, 3ème violon (élémentaire), 4ème violon (à la place de l'alto), alto, violoncelle et contrebasse.
   * Disponibles aussi avec les parties supplémentaires de bois, cuivres et percussions.

Tutti questi pezzi sono disponibili per pianoforte, primo violino, secondo violino, terzo violino semplice, quarto violino (al posto della viola), viola, violoncello e contrabasso.
   * anche con parti aggiuntive per strumenti a fiato, ottoni e strumenti a percussione.

これらはすべて，ピアノ，第1バイオリン，第2バイオリン，
第3エリメンタリー・バイオリン，第4バイオリン，ビオラ，
チェロ，ダブルベースのパート付きです。

＊ウッドウインド，ブラス，パーカッションのパートもあります。

**BOSWORTH**